EMMANUEL JOSEPH

From Davos to Dubai, The Billionaires Who Move Countries and Markets

Copyright © 2025 by Emmanuel Joseph

All rights reserved. No part of this publication may be reproduced, stored or transmitted in any form or by any means, electronic, mechanical, photocopying, recording, scanning, or otherwise without written permission from the publisher. It is illegal to copy this book, post it to a website, or distribute it by any other means without permission.

First edition

This book was professionally typeset on Reedsy.
Find out more at reedsy.com

Contents

1	Chapter 1: The Birth of Wealth	1
2	Chapter 2: The Power of Networking	3
3	Chapter 3: The Influence of Innovation	5
4	Chapter 4: The Global Footprint	7
5	Chapter 5: The Rise of New Economies	9
6	Chapter 6: The Politics of Wealth	11
7	Chapter 7: The Art of Deal-Making	13
8	Chapter 8: The Role of Philanthropy	15
9	Chapter 9: The Impact of Technology	17
10	Chapter 10: The Luxury of Leisure	19
11	Chapter 11: The Pursuit of Power	21
12	Chapter 12: The Legacy of Wealth	23
13	Chapter 13: The Ethics of Wealth	25
14	Chapter 14: The Future of Wealth	27
15	Chapter 15: The Human Side of Wealth	29
16	Chapter 16: The Resilience of Wealth	31
17	Chapter 17: The Legacy Continues	33

1

Chapter 1: The Birth of Wealth

The world of the ultra-wealthy begins with a spark of genius, innovation, or sometimes sheer determination. In the early years of capitalism, industrial magnates like Andrew Carnegie and John D. Rockefeller built empires from steel and oil, laying the foundations for modern wealth accumulation. Their legacies live on today, inspiring a new generation of billionaires who seek to not only amass fortunes but also to shape the world in their image. As we delve into the stories of these modern titans, we see a recurring theme: the convergence of opportunity, vision, and relentless drive.

The advent of technology in the late 20th and early 21st centuries ushered in a new era of wealth creation. Visionaries like Bill Gates and Steve Jobs revolutionized personal computing, while Jeff Bezos and Elon Musk redefined commerce and transportation. These tech moguls leveraged the digital age to build colossal enterprises, creating immense wealth in the process. Their impact extends far beyond their industries, influencing global markets and economies in profound ways.

With great wealth comes great responsibility, and many billionaires have embraced the challenge of philanthropy. Inspired by the likes of Andrew Carnegie, who famously advocated for the redistribution of wealth, modern philanthropists like Warren Buffett and Mark Zuckerberg have pledged significant portions of their fortunes to charitable causes. Through their foundations and initiatives, they address pressing global issues, from education and healthcare to climate change and social justice. Their efforts demonstrate a commitment to leaving a positive legacy and making the world a better place.

However, the accumulation of vast wealth is not without its controversies. Critics argue that the concentration of wealth in the hands of a few exacerbates economic inequality and undermines democratic processes. The influence of billionaires in politics and policy-making raises concerns about the balance of power in society. As we explore the lives of these influential figures, we must also consider the broader implications of their actions and the ethical dilemmas they face. In the following chapters, we will delve deeper into the stories of these billionaires, examining their triumphs, challenges, and the impact they have on the world.

2

Chapter 2: The Power of Networking

In the realm of the ultra-wealthy, connections are currency. The Davos World Economic Forum, held annually in the Swiss Alps, is a prime example of how billionaires leverage their networks to influence global events. This exclusive gathering brings together political leaders, business magnates, and thought leaders to discuss and shape the future of the world. The power of networking at Davos cannot be overstated, as deals are struck, partnerships are formed, and policies are influenced behind closed doors.

Networking is not just about attending high-profile events; it's about building and maintaining relationships. Billionaires often cultivate networks of advisors, mentors, and peers who provide valuable insights and support. For instance, Warren Buffett's long-standing friendship with fellow billionaire Bill Gates has led to significant philanthropic collaborations through the Bill & Melinda Gates Foundation. These relationships are built on mutual respect, trust, and shared values, creating a powerful web of influence that extends across industries and continents.

The digital age has also transformed the landscape of networking. Social media platforms, professional networks, and virtual conferences have made it easier for billionaires to connect with like-minded individuals and stay informed about global trends. Elon Musk, for example, uses Twitter not only to communicate with his followers but also to engage with industry experts, policymakers, and other influential figures. This digital connectivity enhances their ability to shape public opinion, drive innovation, and respond to emerging challenges.

However, the power of networking also comes with its challenges. The concentration of influence within elite circles can lead to an insular worldview and a disconnect from the broader population. Critics argue that the close-knit nature of billionaire networks perpetuates inequality and reinforces the status quo. As we continue our exploration of these influential figures, we will examine how they navigate the complexities of their networks and the impact of their connections on the world.

3

Chapter 3: The Influence of Innovation

Innovation is the lifeblood of wealth creation, and billionaires are often at the forefront of pioneering new technologies and business models. From Silicon Valley to Shenzhen, these visionaries drive progress and disrupt established industries. The stories of tech moguls like Elon Musk and Jeff Bezos exemplify the transformative power of innovation, as they push the boundaries of what's possible and redefine the future of transportation, space exploration, and commerce.

Elon Musk, the founder of Tesla and SpaceX, is a prime example of how innovation can create immense wealth and reshape entire industries. His vision of a sustainable future has driven the development of electric vehicles, solar energy solutions, and ambitious space missions. Musk's relentless pursuit of groundbreaking technologies has made him one of the most influential figures of our time, inspiring a new generation of entrepreneurs to think big and challenge the status quo.

Jeff Bezos, the founder of Amazon, revolutionized the way we shop and consume goods. His relentless focus on customer satisfaction and operational efficiency has turned Amazon into one of the largest and most valuable companies in the world. Bezos's innovative approach to e-commerce, logistics, and cloud computing has had a profound impact on global markets, creating new opportunities for businesses and consumers alike. His story is a testament to the power of vision and perseverance in the face of adversity.

Innovation is not limited to technology; it extends to finance, healthcare, and other industries as well. Billionaires like Warren Buffett and Bill Gates have leveraged their wealth and influence to drive innovation in philanthropy and social impact. Through their foundations, they support cutting-edge research, invest in innovative solutions, and advocate for systemic change. Their efforts demonstrate that innovation can be a powerful force for good, addressing some of the world's most pressing challenges and improving the lives of millions.

The influence of innovation is not without its controversies. The rapid pace of technological change raises ethical and societal questions, such as the impact of automation on jobs, data privacy concerns, and the digital divide. As we continue our exploration of these influential figures, we will delve deeper into the complexities of innovation and the responsibilities that come with it.

4

Chapter 4: The Global Footprint

The wealth and influence of billionaires know no borders. These individuals often operate on a global scale, with business interests and investments spanning multiple countries and continents. The interconnectedness of the global economy means that their actions can have far-reaching consequences, impacting markets, industries, and even nations. This chapter explores how billionaires navigate the complexities of the global landscape and leverage their resources to shape the world.

One of the key aspects of the global footprint of billionaires is their ability to move capital and resources across borders. This mobility allows them to take advantage of favorable economic conditions, tax incentives, and regulatory environments. For instance, many tech giants have established operations in countries with lower tax rates to maximize their profits. This practice, while legal, has sparked debates about tax fairness and the responsibilities of multinational corporations.

Billionaires also play a significant role in shaping international trade and investment. Through their business ventures, they create jobs, stimulate economic growth, and foster innovation. Companies like Alibaba, led by Jack Ma, have transformed e-commerce in China and expanded their reach to global markets. These ventures not only generate wealth but also contribute to the development of infrastructure, education, and healthcare in the regions where they operate.

Philanthropy is another way in which billionaires make a global impact. Through their charitable foundations, they support initiatives that address pressing global issues, such as poverty, disease, and environmental sustainability. The Bill & Melinda Gates Foundation, for example, has made significant contributions to global health, funding research and programs to combat diseases like malaria, HIV/AIDS, and tuberculosis. These philanthropic efforts demonstrate the potential of wealth to drive positive change on a global scale.

However, the global footprint of billionaires is not without controversy. Critics argue that their influence can undermine local economies, exacerbate inequality, and perpetuate a concentration of power. The rise of global elites has raised questions about accountability, governance, and the balance of power in the international system. As we continue our exploration of these influential figures, we will examine the complexities of their global impact and the ethical considerations that arise.

5

Chapter 5: The Rise of New Economies

The global landscape of wealth and power is constantly evolving, with emerging economies playing an increasingly important role. Countries like China, India, and Brazil have become major players on the world stage, producing a new generation of billionaires who are shaping the future. This chapter explores the rise of these new economies and the influential figures driving their growth.

China's rapid economic growth has been one of the most significant developments of the past few decades. Visionary entrepreneurs like Jack Ma and Pony Ma have built tech giants like Alibaba and Tencent, transforming the way people shop, communicate, and access information. These companies have not only created immense wealth but also driven innovation and economic development in China and beyond. The rise of China's tech industry has positioned the country as a global leader in technology and e-commerce.

India, too, has seen a surge in entrepreneurial activity, with billionaires like Mukesh Ambani and Azim Premji leading the charge. Ambani's Reliance Industries has diversified into various sectors, including telecommunications, retail, and petrochemicals, driving economic growth and job creation. Premji, through his company Wipro, has played a pivotal role in the growth of India's IT industry, making the country a global hub for technology and outsourcing services. These entrepreneurs have not only created wealth but also contributed to India's economic transformation.

Brazil, with its abundant natural resources and growing consumer market, has also produced influential billionaires. Figures like Jorge Paulo Lemann have built empires in the beverage and retail industries, driving economic growth and investment in the country. Lemann's 3G Capital has been involved in high-profile mergers and acquisitions, reshaping global industries and creating new opportunities for businesses and consumers.

The rise of new economies presents both opportunities and challenges. While these countries have experienced significant economic growth, they also face issues like inequality, corruption, and environmental sustainability. The actions of their billionaires can have profound implications for their development trajectories. As we continue our exploration of these influential figures, we will examine how they navigate the complexities of emerging economies and the impact of their actions on the global stage.

6

Chapter 6: The Politics of Wealth

The intersection of wealth and politics is a complex and often contentious arena. Billionaires wield significant influence over political processes, shaping policies and decisions that impact society at large. This chapter delves into the ways in which the ultra-wealthy engage with politics and the implications of their involvement.

Political donations and lobbying are common strategies employed by billionaires to advance their interests. In the United States, figures like Sheldon Adelson and Michael Bloomberg have used their wealth to support political candidates and causes that align with their values and business interests. These contributions can sway elections, shape policy agendas, and influence legislative outcomes. The power of money in politics raises questions about the integrity of democratic processes and the balance of power in society.

Billionaires also engage in direct political participation, with some choosing to run for public office. Donald Trump, the real estate mogul and former president of the United States, is a notable example of a billionaire who transitioned from the business world to the political arena. His presidency highlighted the ways in which wealth and business acumen can influence governance and policy-making. Other billionaires, like Silvio Berlusconi in Italy and Andrej Babiš in the Czech Republic, have also pursued political careers, leveraging their business success to gain political power.

Philanthropy is another avenue through which billionaires influence politics. By funding think tanks, advocacy groups, and social movements, they shape public discourse and drive policy change. The Koch brothers, Charles and David, have been known for their extensive network of organizations that promote free-market policies and conservative values. Similarly, George Soros's Open Society Foundations support initiatives that promote democracy, human rights, and social justice around the world.

The involvement of billionaires in politics is not without its controversies. Critics argue that their influence can undermine democratic processes, perpetuate inequality, and prioritize the interests of the wealthy over the common good. The concentration of power in the hands of a few raises concerns about accountability, transparency, and the potential for conflicts of interest. As we continue our exploration of these influential figures, we will examine the complexities of their political engagement and the ethical considerations it entails.

7

Chapter 7: The Art of Deal-Making

Deal-making is an essential skill for billionaires, enabling them to expand their empires and secure their positions at the top. This chapter delves into the strategies and tactics employed by the ultra-wealthy to negotiate and close deals that shape industries and markets. From mergers and acquisitions to strategic partnerships, the art of deal-making is a critical component of their success.

One of the most famous deal-makers in recent history is Warren Buffett, the chairman and CEO of Berkshire Hathaway. Known for his value investing approach, Buffett has built a reputation for making shrewd investments in undervalued companies. His acquisition of companies like GEICO, Dairy Queen, and BNSF Railway has solidified Berkshire Hathaway's position as a conglomerate with diverse interests. Buffett's ability to identify opportunities and negotiate favorable terms has made him one of the most respected figures in the business world.

Another notable deal-maker is Elon Musk, whose bold and ambitious approach to business has led to groundbreaking ventures. Musk's acquisition of SolarCity and its integration into Tesla exemplifies his strategic vision and ability to execute complex deals. By combining solar energy solutions with electric vehicles, Musk has created a vertically integrated company that addresses multiple aspects of sustainable energy. His willingness to take risks and pursue unconventional strategies has set him apart as a visionary entrepreneur.

Deal-making is not limited to the business world; it also extends to philanthropy and social impact. Billionaires like Bill Gates and Melinda French Gates have used their wealth and influence to forge partnerships with governments, NGOs, and other organizations to address global challenges. The Bill & Melinda Gates Foundation's collaboration with Gavi, the Vaccine Alliance, is a prime example of how strategic partnerships can drive significant progress in public health. By leveraging their resources and networks, they have helped to improve vaccination rates and save millions of lives.

However, the art of deal-making is not without its challenges. Negotiations can be complex and fraught with obstacles, requiring a deep understanding of market dynamics, legal considerations, and human psychology. The stakes are high, and the consequences of a failed deal can be significant. As we continue our exploration of these influential figures, we will examine the intricacies of their deal-making strategies and the impact of their decisions on the world.

8

Chapter 8: The Role of Philanthropy

Philanthropy is a defining characteristic of many billionaires, reflecting their desire to give back to society and address pressing global issues. This chapter explores the motivations, strategies, and impact of philanthropic efforts by the ultra-wealthy. From funding education and healthcare initiatives to supporting environmental sustainability, philanthropy plays a crucial role in shaping the legacy of billionaires.

One of the most prominent philanthropists of our time is Bill Gates, whose foundation has made significant contributions to global health and development. The Bill & Melinda Gates Foundation focuses on areas such as infectious disease control, poverty alleviation, and education. Through strategic investments and partnerships, the foundation has achieved remarkable results, including the near-eradication of polio and significant progress in malaria prevention. Gates's commitment to philanthropy demonstrates the potential of wealth to drive positive change on a global scale.

Another influential philanthropist is Warren Buffett, who has pledged to give away the majority of his fortune to charitable causes. Buffett's approach to philanthropy is characterized by his emphasis on long-term impact and sustainability. He has donated billions of dollars to the Bill & Melinda Gates Foundation and other organizations, supporting initiatives that address critical issues such as poverty, education, and healthcare. Buffett's philanthropic philosophy is rooted in the belief that wealth should be used to improve the lives of others and create a better world.

Philanthropy is not limited to financial contributions; it also involves the use of influence and expertise to drive change. Billionaires like Michael Bloomberg have leveraged their business acumen and networks to advocate for policies and initiatives that promote public health, environmental sustainability, and social justice. Bloomberg's philanthropic efforts include funding anti-tobacco campaigns, supporting climate action, and promoting gun safety measures. His approach demonstrates the power of combining financial resources with strategic advocacy to achieve meaningful impact.

However, the role of philanthropy is not without its controversies. Critics argue that the concentration of philanthropic power in the hands of a few can undermine democratic processes and perpetuate inequality. The influence of billionaires in shaping public policy and priorities raises questions about accountability and transparency. As we continue our exploration of these influential figures, we will examine the complexities of their philanthropic efforts and the ethical considerations they entail.

9

Chapter 9: The Impact of Technology

Technology is a driving force behind the wealth and influence of many billionaires, shaping industries and transforming societies. This chapter delves into the ways in which technological advancements have created opportunities for wealth creation and the impact of these innovations on the world. From the rise of the internet to the advent of artificial intelligence, technology has revolutionized the way we live, work, and interact.

The internet has been one of the most transformative technologies of the past few decades, creating new opportunities for entrepreneurs and businesses. Visionaries like Jeff Bezos and Mark Zuckerberg have harnessed the power of the internet to build global empires. Amazon, founded by Bezos, has revolutionized e-commerce, logistics, and cloud computing, becoming one of the most valuable companies in the world. Facebook, founded by Zuckerberg, has transformed the way people connect and share information, creating a platform with billions of users worldwide. These tech giants have not only created immense wealth but also reshaped entire industries and changed the way we interact with technology.

Artificial intelligence (AI) is another area where billionaires are driving innovation and creating new opportunities. Elon Musk, through his company Neuralink, is exploring the potential of AI to enhance human capabilities and address neurological disorders. His vision of a future where humans and AI coexist and collaborate has the potential to revolutionize healthcare, education, and other sectors. Similarly, companies like Google and Microsoft are investing heavily in AI research and development, pushing the boundaries of what is possible and creating new opportunities for businesses and consumers.

The impact of technology extends beyond business and commerce; it also has profound implications for society and the environment. Technological advancements have the potential to address some of the world's most pressing challenges, from climate change to healthcare. For example, renewable energy technologies, such as solar and wind power, are driving the transition to a more sustainable energy future. Innovations in healthcare, such as telemedicine and personalized medicine, are improving access to care and patient outcomes. These advancements demonstrate the potential of technology to create a better world.

However, the rapid pace of technological change also raises ethical and societal questions. Issues such as data privacy, cybersecurity, and the digital divide highlight the need for responsible innovation and regulation. As we continue our exploration of these influential figures, we will examine the complexities of their technological endeavors and the responsibilities that come with their innovations.

10

Chapter 10: The Luxury of Leisure

While the lives of billionaires are often characterized by relentless drive and ambition, they also indulge in the luxury of leisure. This chapter explores how the ultra-wealthy spend their leisure time, from extravagant vacations to collecting rare art and investing in exclusive hobbies. The pursuit of leisure is not just about relaxation; it also reflects their tastes, interests, and the ways in which they seek to create unique experiences.

Travel is a common pursuit for billionaires, who often have the means to explore the world's most luxurious destinations. Private jets, yachts, and exclusive resorts provide them with unparalleled comfort and privacy. Destinations like the French Riviera, the Maldives, and the Caribbean are popular among the ultra-wealthy, offering pristine beaches, world-class amenities, and a sense of exclusivity. These travel experiences are not just about luxury; they also provide opportunities for networking, business discussions, and exploring new investment opportunities.

Art collecting is another popular leisure activity among billionaires. Figures like Eli Broad and Leonard Lauder have amassed impressive art collections that span centuries and genres. These collections not only reflect their personal tastes but also serve as valuable investments. Art fairs, auctions, and galleries provide venues for billionaires to acquire and showcase their collections. The art world offers a unique blend of culture, history, and prestige, making it an attractive pursuit for the wealthy.

Hobbies and passions also play a significant role in the leisure activities of billionaires. For example, Richard Branson, the founder of the Virgin Group, is known for his adventurous spirit and love of extreme sports. From hot air ballooning to space tourism, Branson's pursuits reflect his desire to push boundaries and explore new frontiers. Similarly, tech mogul Larry Ellison has a passion for sailing, having invested in competitive yacht racing and owning one of the world's most advanced sailing yachts.

The luxury of leisure is not without its challenges. The public scrutiny of their lavish lifestyles can lead to criticism and backlash, particularly in times of economic hardship. The pursuit of exclusive experiences can also create a sense of isolation, as the ultra-wealthy move in circles that are often disconnected from the broader population. As we continue our exploration of these influential figures, we will examine the complexities of their leisure activities and the ways in which they seek to balance their pursuit of luxury with their responsibilities.

11

Chapter 11: The Pursuit of Power

For many billionaires, the accumulation of wealth is closely tied to the pursuit of power. This chapter delves into the ways in which the ultra-wealthy seek to influence and shape the world, from political engagement to control over media and public opinion. The pursuit of power is a complex and multifaceted endeavor, reflecting their desire to leave a lasting legacy and make a significant impact.

One of the most direct ways billionaires exert power is through political engagement. As previously discussed, political donations, lobbying, and running for public office are common strategies employed by the ultra-wealthy to influence policy and governance. Figures like Michael Bloomberg and George Soros have used their wealth to advocate for causes they believe in, shaping public discourse and driving policy change. Their involvement in politics reflects a desire to leverage their resources and expertise to address societal challenges and promote their vision of a better world.

Control over media is another avenue through which billionaires exert power. Media moguls like Rupert Murdoch and Jeff Bezos have significant influence over the dissemination of information and the shaping of public opinion. Murdoch's News Corp and its subsidiaries, including Fox News and The Wall Street Journal, play a pivotal role in shaping political and cultural narratives. Similarly, Bezos's ownership of The Washington Post has positioned him as a key player in the media landscape. The power of media control highlights the ways in which billionaires can shape public perception and influence the agenda.

The pursuit of power also extends to the realm of business and industry. Through their companies, billionaires create jobs, drive economic growth, and shape markets. Their decisions have far-reaching consequences, impacting employees, consumers, and communities. The influence of billionaires in the corporate world raises questions about accountability, governance, and the balance of power between shareholders, stakeholders, and society at large.

However, the pursuit of power is not without its controversies. Critics argue that the concentration of power in the hands of a few can undermine democratic processes, perpetuate inequality, and prioritize the interests of the wealthy over the common good. The influence of billionaires in politics, media, and business raises ethical considerations and challenges the notion of a level playing field. As we continue our exploration of these influential figures, we will examine the complexities of their pursuit of power and the impact of their actions on society.

12

Chapter 12: The Legacy of Wealth

The legacy of wealth is a central concern for many billionaires, reflecting their desire to leave a lasting impact on the world. This chapter explores the ways in which the ultra-wealthy seek to shape their legacies, from philanthropy and social impact to succession planning and the preservation of their empires. The legacy of wealth is not just about financial success; it is also about the values, principles, and contributions that define their lives.

Philanthropy is a key component of the legacy of many billionaires. Through their charitable foundations and initiatives, they seek to address pressing global challenges and make a positive difference in the world. Figures like Bill Gates, Warren Buffett, and George Soros have committed significant portions of their fortunes to philanthropic causes, supporting initiatives in areas such as health, education, and social justice. Their philanthropic efforts reflect a desire to use their wealth for the greater good and leave a positive legacy.

Succession planning is another important aspect of preserving the legacy of wealth. Ensuring the continuity of their businesses and investments is a priority for many billionaires, who often involve their families in their enterprises. For example, the Walton family, heirs to the Walmart fortune, have maintained control of the company through careful succession planning and governance structures. Similarly, the Murdoch family has played a central role in the management and direction of News Corp. The preservation of wealth and influence across generations reflects a desire to maintain their legacy and ensure the continued success of their endeavors.

The legacy of wealth also extends to the preservation of cultural and historical heritage. Many billionaires invest in the arts, museums, and cultural institutions, seeking to preserve and promote culture and knowledge. The Getty family's contributions to art and cultural preservation through the J. Paul Getty Trust and the Getty Museum are a notable example of how wealth can be used to support cultural initiatives. These efforts reflect a commitment to preserving the richness of human history and creativity for future generations.

However, the legacy of wealth is not without its challenges. The concentration of wealth and influence raises questions about inequality, accountability, and the responsibilities of the ultra-wealthy. The ethical considerations of wealth accumulation and its impact on society are complex and multifaceted. As we continue our exploration of these influential figures, we will examine the ways in which they seek to shape their legacies and the broader implications of their actions.

13

Chapter 13: The Ethics of Wealth

The accumulation of vast wealth by billionaires raises important ethical questions about fairness, responsibility, and the impact of their actions on society. This chapter delves into the ethical considerations that arise from the concentration of wealth and power in the hands of a few. From income inequality to corporate responsibility, the ethics of wealth is a complex and multifaceted issue that requires careful examination.

Income inequality is one of the most pressing ethical concerns associated with billionaire wealth. The gap between the ultra-wealthy and the rest of the population has been widening, leading to disparities in access to resources, opportunities, and social mobility. Critics argue that the concentration of wealth in the hands of a few undermines social cohesion and exacerbates economic inequality. Addressing these disparities requires a nuanced understanding of the underlying factors and the development of policies that promote equitable growth and opportunity for all.

Corporate responsibility is another important ethical consideration for billionaires. As leaders of major corporations, they have a duty to ensure that their businesses operate in a manner that is socially and environmentally responsible. This includes addressing issues such as labor rights, environmental sustainability, and ethical supply chain practices. For example, companies like Patagonia and Ben & Jerry's have made significant efforts to incorporate social and environmental responsibility into their business models, setting an example for others to follow.

Philanthropy can also raise ethical questions, particularly when it comes to the influence of billionaire donors on public policy and social priorities. While philanthropic efforts can drive positive change, there is a risk that the priorities of wealthy individuals may not align with the needs and interests of the broader population. The concentration of philanthropic power in the hands of a few can lead to concerns about accountability and transparency. Ensuring that philanthropic efforts are inclusive, equitable, and aligned with the needs of communities is essential for addressing these ethical challenges.

The role of government and regulation is crucial in addressing the ethical considerations associated with billionaire wealth. Policymakers must develop frameworks that promote transparency, accountability, and fairness in wealth accumulation and distribution. This includes addressing issues such as tax fairness, corporate governance, and anti-trust regulations. By creating an environment that fosters responsible wealth creation and addresses disparities, governments can help to ensure that the benefits of economic growth are shared more broadly.

14

Chapter 14: The Future of Wealth

The landscape of wealth and influence is constantly evolving, shaped by technological advancements, economic trends, and societal changes. This chapter explores the future of wealth, examining the emerging trends and challenges that will define the next generation of billionaires. From the rise of new industries to the impact of climate change, the future of wealth is a dynamic and multifaceted topic.

One of the most significant trends shaping the future of wealth is the rise of new industries and technologies. Fields such as artificial intelligence, biotechnology, and renewable energy are poised to create new opportunities for wealth creation and innovation. Entrepreneurs and investors who can capitalize on these emerging trends will likely become the next generation of billionaires. For example, the development of autonomous vehicles, advanced robotics, and sustainable energy solutions has the potential to revolutionize industries and create significant economic value.

The impact of climate change is another critical factor that will shape the future of wealth. As the world grapples with the challenges of environmental sustainability, there will be opportunities for innovation and investment in green technologies and solutions. Billionaires who invest in renewable energy, sustainable agriculture, and climate resilience initiatives will play a crucial role in driving the transition to a more sustainable future. The intersection of wealth and environmental responsibility will be a defining feature of the next generation of influential figures.

The future of wealth is also influenced by changing societal values and expectations. There is a growing emphasis on social responsibility, ethical business practices, and inclusive growth. Billionaires who can align their business strategies and philanthropic efforts with these values will be better positioned to navigate the complexities of the modern world. The rise of impact investing, corporate social responsibility, and ethical entrepreneurship reflects a broader shift towards a more conscious and sustainable approach to wealth creation.

However, the future of wealth is not without its challenges. Issues such as income inequality, geopolitical instability, and technological disruption will continue to pose significant risks and uncertainties. Addressing these challenges requires a proactive and adaptive approach, with a focus on creating inclusive and equitable opportunities for all. As we continue our exploration of these influential figures, we will examine how they navigate the uncertainties of the future and the impact of their actions on the world.

15

Chapter 15: The Human Side of Wealth

While the accumulation of wealth and influence is often the focus of attention, it is important to recognize the human side of billionaires. This chapter explores the personal stories, struggles, and triumphs of the ultra-wealthy, shedding light on the complexities and challenges they face. From family dynamics to personal values, the human side of wealth reveals the multifaceted nature of these influential figures.

Family dynamics play a significant role in the lives of billionaires, shaping their decisions, priorities, and legacies. Balancing the demands of business and family life can be challenging, and the pressures of wealth can strain relationships. For example, the Walton family, heirs to the Walmart fortune, have faced challenges in managing their wealth and maintaining family unity. Similarly, the complexities of succession planning and generational transitions can create tensions and conflicts within wealthy families.

Personal values and principles also shape the actions and decisions of billionaires. Many influential figures are driven by a sense of purpose and a desire to make a positive impact on the world. For example, philanthropists like Bill and Melinda Gates are motivated by their commitment to improving global health and reducing poverty. Their philanthropic efforts reflect their values and the belief that wealth should be used to address pressing social challenges. Understanding the personal motivations and values of billionaires provides insight into the complexities of their actions and decisions.

The human side of wealth also includes the personal struggles and challenges faced by billionaires. Despite their immense resources, they are not immune to the pressures and stresses of life. Issues such as mental health, work-life balance, and public scrutiny can take a toll on their well-being. Recognizing the human side of wealth reminds us that billionaires, like everyone else, face a range of personal challenges and complexities.

The stories of the ultra-wealthy are a reminder of the multifaceted nature of wealth and influence. While their financial success and public profiles often dominate the narrative, it is important to acknowledge the human side of their journeys. As we continue our exploration of these influential figures, we will delve deeper into the personal stories and experiences that shape their lives.

16

Chapter 16: The Resilience of Wealth

The resilience of wealth is a testament to the ability of billionaires to adapt and thrive in the face of adversity. This chapter explores how the ultra-wealthy navigate economic downturns, market fluctuations, and personal challenges to maintain and grow their wealth. The stories of resilience and recovery offer valuable insights into the strategies and mindsets that enable billionaires to overcome obstacles and emerge stronger.

Economic downturns and market fluctuations are inevitable, and billionaires must be prepared to navigate these challenges. The financial crisis of 2008, for example, tested the resilience of many wealthy individuals and their businesses. Warren Buffett, known for his value investing approach, demonstrated his ability to weather the storm by making strategic investments in companies like Goldman Sachs and General Electric. His calm and measured approach during times of crisis has earned him a reputation as a savvy and resilient investor.

Personal challenges and setbacks are also a part of the journey for many billionaires. The ability to overcome adversity and learn from failures is a key trait that sets them apart. For example, Steve Jobs faced numerous challenges throughout his career, including being ousted from Apple, the company he co-founded. However, his resilience and determination led him to create NeXT and Pixar, both of which achieved significant success. Jobs's eventual return to Apple and the company's resurgence under his leadership are a testament to his resilience and visionary approach.

Innovation and adaptability are crucial for maintaining resilience in the face of changing circumstances. Billionaires who can anticipate and respond to emerging trends and disruptions are better positioned to thrive. Elon Musk, for example, has demonstrated his ability to pivot and adapt his ventures to changing market dynamics. His focus on innovation and long-term vision has enabled him to navigate challenges and drive the success of companies like Tesla and SpaceX.

The resilience of wealth is not just about financial success; it also involves the ability to maintain personal well-being and a sense of purpose. Balancing the demands of business and personal life, managing stress, and staying true to one's values are important aspects of resilience. As we continue our exploration of these influential figures, we will examine the strategies and mindsets that enable them to navigate adversity and maintain their resilience.

17

Chapter 17: The Legacy Continues

As we reach the final chapter of our exploration, we reflect on the enduring legacy of the billionaires who have shaped our world. The stories of these influential figures offer valuable lessons and insights into the nature of wealth, power, and influence. Their journeys are a reminder of the complexities and responsibilities that come with great wealth and the potential to drive positive change.

The legacy of billionaires is multifaceted, encompassing their financial success, philanthropic efforts, and contributions to society. Figures like Bill Gates, Warren Buffett, and Elon Musk have left an indelible mark on the world, inspiring future generations of entrepreneurs and leaders. Their stories highlight the importance of vision, innovation, and resilience in achieving success and making a lasting impact.

As we look to the future, the next generation of billionaires will continue to shape our world in new and exciting ways. Emerging industries, technological advancements, and changing societal values will create new opportunities and challenges. The ability to navigate these dynamics and drive positive change will be a defining characteristic of the future of wealth.

The stories of the ultra-wealthy also remind us of the importance of ethical considerations and social responsibility. The impact of their actions on society, the environment, and the broader population underscores the need for a balanced and inclusive approach to wealth creation. By embracing their responsibilities and leveraging their resources for the greater good, billionaires have the potential to create a better and more equitable world.

As we conclude our exploration of these influential figures, we are reminded of the power of wealth to shape our world and the importance of using that power responsibly. The legacy of billionaires is a testament to the potential of human ingenuity, vision, and determination to drive progress and create positive change.

Book Description

From Davos to Dubai: The Billionaires Who Move Countries and Markets

In this captivating exploration, "From Davos to Dubai: The Billionaires Who Move Countries and Markets" delves into the lives of the world's most influential figures. These billionaires, who have amassed immense wealth and power, shape economies, drive innovation, and influence global events.

This book takes readers on a journey through the stories of visionary entrepreneurs, tech moguls, and philanthropic leaders who have left an indelible mark on the world. From the birth of modern wealth in the industrial age to the rise of new economies and technological advancements, each chapter offers a detailed and engaging narrative of how these individuals have transformed industries and markets.

Readers will gain insights into the power of networking, the art of deal-making, and the role of philanthropy in shaping the legacy of the ultra-wealthy. The book also addresses the ethical considerations and societal impact of concentrated wealth, highlighting the responsibilities and challenges faced by billionaires in the modern world.

As we look to the future, "From Davos to Dubai" examines emerging trends and the next generation of influential figures who will continue to shape our world. With a focus on resilience, innovation, and social responsibility, this book offers a comprehensive and thought-provoking exploration of the billionaires who move countries and markets.

www.ingramcontent.com/pod-product-compliance
Lightning Source LLC
LaVergne TN
LVHW020458080526
838202LV00057B/6016